T0033350

FOR THE SHREW
для землеройки

FOR THE SHREW
для землеройки

POEMS BY

Anna Glazova

TRANSLATED FROM RUSSIAN BY

Alex Niemi

Zephyr Press

This publication is made possible in part by the Academy of American Poets
with funds from the Amazon Literary Partnership Poetry Fund.

Zephyr Press acknowledges with gratitude the continuing financial support
of the Massachusetts Cultural Council.

Zephyr Press, a non-profit arts and education 501(c)(3) organization, publishes
literary titles that foster a deeper understanding of cultures and languages.
Zephyr Press books are distributed to the trade by Consortium Book Sales
and Distribution [www.cbsd.com].

Cataloguing-in publication data is available from the Library of Congress.

ZEPHYR PRESS
www.zephyrpress.org

TABLE OF CONTENTS

Часть полноты | Part of a Whole

On the Boundaries of Conversation | Anna Glazova

Much of what is said between people is spoken only *for* people. Even the idea of speaking to a non-person may seem wild at first, since "wild" is the word we use for everything that isn't defined by human experience. However, we aren't surprised when people speak to animals, plants, or even nonliving things. A pet might have a human name or listen to its owner's complaints about life, and people often say that objects "tell the story" of their owners. Children are especially open-minded about speaking with creatures and objects, and they can bestow a soul on anything from a toy animal to the pillows on a couch. The boundaries of conversation between people don't exhaust our receptivity to communication, not only concerning human language, but language as such. It's easy to forget about the openness of communication in the routine of daily conversation.

Openness is easier to achieve in poetry, though as a form of communication it can be more difficult to process. Poetry has no direct, practical goal; it doesn't convey information so much as— in the broadest sense—convey a state of being. The basic function of language may be communication, meaning an exchange of information, but the possibilities of language are much broader, and poetry exists in a sphere of language where communication is not indisputably the highest power. In poetry, it is possible to have a noncommunicative reader. Addressing this reader in poetic speech is easier than addressing someone you already know through a poem, as the imagined noncommunicative reader is a broader and more flexible concept.

Почти в обратную сторону

Almost backwards

*

знал бы,
кого затянуло
в пустую точку на стекле без отблеска.

ветка бьёт в крышу где-то там сзади.
это он не смотрит а видит узость зрения.

и что теперь? вставай если можешь тебе всего хватает.
не вставай если не гложет. кого-то несёт, другой заработал хромоту,
каждый трудом отражает память что всё стоит.

(видано и беглецов

худых на вечном подъёме.

не ждёт ни бутылка воды ни попутный поезд.)

верхом твоими же ногами на холме;
а другой и в грязных пелёнках
не выучил
о следствии ходьбы.

*

if he'd only known,
who was pulled
to an empty point in the opaque glass.

a branch is smacking the roof somewhere in back.
he's the one, not observing, but seeing the narrowness of vision.

what now? get up if you can you have what you need.
don't if you can't feel the gnawing. someone is carried, another earns a limp,
each person struggles to reflect the memory of everything standing still,

(thin refugees seen

on an eternal ascent.

neither a bottle of water nor the right train awaits you.)

astride your own two legs on a hill;
another in dirty diapers by now
never learned enough
about the consequences of walking.

*

Полине Барсковой

в лакуне

из голодного теста
лежит,
втиснута,

красным домом
яичная скорлупа;

нам
дан этот день,

«Кто *мы*?,

Подошло! Подошло!»

*

for Polina Barskova

in a space

formed by hungry dough
lies,
crammed,

an eggshell
like a red house;

they gave us
this day,

"Who *are* we?

Here to serve! Here to serve!"

*

тёмный и влажный оттиск
над дрожью над связью
рук у развилки.

тогдашние реки: здесь,
капля,
ты решилась
нырнуть на дно и там
высохнуть
с шелестом.

(нас-то и так не больше воды
несло
чем когда выдохнешь
и замёрзнет,
да, я в уме, что хочу из такой паутины
наплести и канат, и гамак,
и опустить, опуститься.)

тёмный
и влажный,
позади вас, развилкой ставшие
руки.

*

a dark, damp impression
above the tremor above the joining
hands of a crossroads.

the rivers from before: here,
a dribble,
you resolved
to dive to the bottom and there
dry off
with a rustle.

(we were carried
by no more water
than a breath frozen in air
when you exhale,
yes, I'm all there, I want to spin
a rope, a hammock of this spider silk,
and drop, descend.)

dark
and damp,
behind you, the hands turned
crossroads.

нас сюда вынесло русло,
вверх дном.

кто-то не видел
кто видел
кто слышал.

a stream brought us here,
upside down.

someone didn't see
who saw
who heard.

полной жизни

в жёлтых тенях стволы груш,
сухие розы и стойкий шиповник,
ими только и держится над ручьём
то что как будто бы твёрдым должно быть,
певчими, а не плавучими птицами,
и к их тонким клювам, блестящим глазам
вода тянется — вязкая, и не удержишь.

радость. не сомну в руке,
не загляну в завязь, когда из-под снега
цветы со мной станут делиться ухваченными лучами,
насмотрюсь лучше на солнце, чтобы всё стало тенью.
стоят чужие стены,
по ту сторону, может быть, идёт разговор, и на ветру
как часы у меня стучит сердце.

of a full life

pear tree trunks dotted with yellow shadows,
dry roses and stalwart briar,
over the brook, they just barely hold on
to what should have been solid,
just barely held by singing, not wading birds —
as viscous water reaches
for their thin beaks and shining eyes — you won't hold out.

joy. I won't crumple in hand,
won't peek into the snow-covered bud,
when flowers share their plucked rays of light,
I stare so long into the sun, that everything else falls into shade.
strange walls rise,
maybe a conversation heard from the other side, and in the wind
my heart strikes like a clock.

*

сплелось из остатков струн — что-то
негодное но целое. сырые
доски, тонкий лак, вообще мастерство
достались кому-то, но звук в снегу не для слуха.

вихрится увиденное,
тяготит грубый напев,
как из скважины брызжет глубокое,
но оно блестит.

— без права голоса, рот,
замкни, запечатай неясность
того, что точно случается неподалёку.

*

woven from leftover string — something
worthless but whole. damp
boards, fine lacquer, a craft alone
is passed down, but a snow-bound sound is not for hearing.

the seen whirls,
the crude tune weighs heavy,
like depths spring from a well,
but it shines.

— no right to a voice, mouth,
lock, seal the lack of clarity
of what obviously happens nearby.

Мёртвые

The Dead

*

всё всегда уже было.
и в тебе, и в земле размешана райская пыль.
ты бы чувствовал боль,
разрезая свой хлеб,
поглотив если бы плакала
свежая наша могила.

*

everything has always happened before.
that edenic dust worked into you and the earth.
you'd have felt pain,
cutting your bread,
swallowed if our fresh
grave were crying.

*

перед рассветом свет упирается в тело и не проходит.
нет сна глубоко как в груди голос.
движение пальцев по воздуху около рта вминает в тело не
                                     живших с тобой
и чистоту под веками среди ночи не видевших вместе с тобой.
их заполняли не ко времени крики себя не помнящей птицы.
нет смысла ждать ума у себя среди ночи
когда те с кем не жил не ложатся как голос в груди в каждый жест
                                     перед дыханием.
знать что все отлегли теперь от твоей жизни.

*

before dawn, light crashes into your body and can't move on.
can't sleep your voice is so deep in your chest.
the play of fingers around your mouth
pressing to your body
the ones who've never lived with you
who've never seen the clarity
behind closed lids with you at midnight.
those spaces filled with the untimely cries of a fickle bird
can't expect much from your mind at night
when the ones who've never lived with you
never lie like a voice in your chest
in each movement before a breath.
know that everyone has left your life at ease.

*

надела свадебные серьги
и всё воскресенье
жгла в раковине
с могилы краденые цветы.

ушла как старуха
из позапрошлого века
с золой и мылом к ручью
тереть об камни бельё,

и вот:
над водой
выжгли брызги
мелкую радугу.

*

she put on the earrings from her wedding
and all Sunday long
stood at the sink burning
flowers stolen from a grave.

she tottered out like an old woman
from two centuries ago
making her way to the stream with soap and ash
to scrub laundry against stone,

and there:
over the water
the spray burned down
to a fragile rainbow.

*

есть слишком глубокой лазурью залитые щели.
в мире ты лёгок как внутри хлеба испарина.

в листьях прожилки в человеке сосуды в сосуде то что хранится.
в удушливой глубине живёт некто оставленный светом.
только из собственных глаз у него свет.
а кто-то и слеп.

у лежащих в земле земля не хлеб и вода.
иногда умолкает и тишина.
не тебя державшие руки в небе просвет.

*

cracks brimming with an azure too deep.
you are light in the world like the steam in fresh bread.

veins of leaves vessels of humans a vessel holds all that you save.
in the airless depths someone lives abandoned by light.
only his eyes shine.
while another is blinded.

earth is not bread or water for those underground.
sometimes even the quiet subsides.
the hands not holding you, the gleam in the sky.

*

как тяжёлое пение из-под земли
запах лопатой разрубленной землеройки
букета и гниющих корней.

вхож ли мой ум скажи в сердце крота
во флакон под стекло
где разложение не истлевает
и *как* растворить голосом голос давно мёртвых
как из желёз выжимки
на коже той или тех, живущих и едва мне смотрящих в глаза?

*

like heavy singing from underground
the smell of a shrew chopped in half by a shovel
a bouquet and moldering roots.

tell me, would my mind fit into the heart of a mole
a vial under glass
where decay never dies
and how do you dissolve voices long dead with your voice
like a glandular distillation on that flesh
or on the flesh of those living barely meeting my gaze?

*

где была пустота после близкого
теперь пелена
как бы ты домотканый саван наплёл.
(а хоронили в готовом платье
но ты туда дотянулся)
как твоё тело и он был соткан из тела.
он давно умер а ты почему-то теперь вспомнил.

когда умер придуманный в книге
умер не живший
после него пустота навсегда гуще
и промочишь бумагу а не замажешь лица.

неизвестный давно мёртвый
убитый может быть
или горем убитый
ты и не знал а носишь на него похожее платье
к нему ты приткнёшься когда умрёшь.

*

the empty space left by a loved one
is now veiled
as if you'd woven a homespun shroud.
(they buried him in store-bought clothes
but you made it there)
woven from a body just like yours.
he died long ago but for some reason
you've just remembered.

when he died imagined in a book
he died unlived
left emptiness forever thicker
and you can soak through the paper
but never blot out that face.

unknown and long dead
maybe killed
or killed by grief
you don't know it, but your clothes are just like his
and he's the one you'll lean on when you die.

*

над предустановленной чашей
клубится гнилой воздух,
глухое согласие
отправленного к отцам.

я могу и с
болотом
стыдливо соединиться,

был бы кто выпил до дна
осевшую муть.

*

putrid air swirls
above the predestined cup,
a dull agreement
sent to fathers.

I can even
bashfully
breed with the swamp,

if there's someone to drink down
the muddy swill.

*

мыкайся горе в моей голове
за слепым пятном за спасением.

или за мутью распался дух
и зовёт: брось меня
если за пылью найдёшь, спрячь
огромное небо
если уж скорбный мимо ума меня туда проглядел.

*

misery, wander in my head
behind that blind spot, after salvation

or that spirit broken in haze
calls: leave me behind
if you find me beyond the dust, hide
the enormous sky
if you, madman, have overlooked me inside

*

отстрадал от души горечавку —
будто сам её видел:

лепестки свёрнуты,
стебли переплетены,
когда лопнут плоды — истекает и оседает на месте.

её, может, и нет, но она мне пишет:

свет бы вернула в глаза,
волну в волосы,

было бы, где разомкнуть, что сомкнулось.

*

suffered the nightshade from his soul —
as if he'd seen it himself:

curled petals,
braided stems,
when the fruit bursts — it oozes and settles into place.

it may not be here, but it writes to me:

I would return the light to your eyes,
the wave to your hair,

if there were a place to open what closed.

*

кто бы не хотел склеиться
из кусочков земли
вывернутых червями
и растений из прошлого
и из сора?

кто бы не хотел сказать,
меня нет,
я ваш должник,
я часть,
мы даже и не мы, а целое?

ты протягиваешь руки,
смотришь,
сажаешь — копаешь,
растишь — строгаешь,

и только когда,
бывает,
задумаешься
до беспамятства,

слышишь вдруг музыку
из того что стало полезным и мёртвым.

*

who wouldn't want to be formed
from clods of earth
pursed with worms,
former plants
and debris?

who wouldn't want to say,
I am not,
I'm your debtor,
a part,
we aren't even we, but a whole?

you stretch out your hands,
you look,
you plant — dig,
you grow — cut,

and only when
you fall
into a reverie
on the verge of delirium,

can you suddenly hear music from this matter
now both useful and dead.

Для землеройки

For the Shrew

*

в голове пчелы
одна
натянута цель —

и она из неё только и тянет мёд,
и медоносы не знают,
и никто,

только что полосы
(так и звук штрихует пространство)
как метроном разделяют
в каждом мае почти каждый луг.

*

in a bee's mind exists
one
taut goal —

and only honey seeps from it,
and sweet nectars don't know,
and no one,

only that stripes
(even the sound draws a line in space)
divide, like a metronome,
every May and in almost every meadow.

*

молния не уходит
когда уже раз побывала в дупле.
в нём осыпается полое место,
и лишайник растёт без воды уже,
насухо, странно, в чёрных стенах.

там поселяются те, кого точно не видно.

и совершаются тайны:
рождение света из ничего
и рождение из мороза.
смерть глубокого тела в котором лежит меховая луна.

*

lightning never leaves
once it's visited the hollow of a tree.
empty space crumbles within,
and lichen begins to grow without water,
dry and strange in the black walls.

those who settle there are precisely those you cannot see.

and mysteries are fulfilled:
birth of light from nothing
and birth from frost.
the death of a deep body holding a furry moon.

*

утверди руку.
буду сидеть над травой как рыбак перед прорубью
и ждать того дня
когда станет трава ископаемым
и тонкая ветка
отзовётся измеренным шёпотом
самому измерению.

*

strengthen the hand.
I'm going to sit over the grass like a fisherman by an ice hole
and wait for the day
when the grass becomes fossilized
and a thin branch
answers in a measured whisper
the call of measurement itself.

*

из перегноя рождается кислый дыхательный воздух.

мы
этой тьмой дышим,
мерно вбирая в свою темноту

тихую смерть
семян и растений.

из всех жизней милее болотная.
быть полужабрами каждой трепетной жабы,
и водомерке на плечи

сложить
тяжёлую душу.

*

humus births the sour air of respiration

we
breathe with this gloom,
rhythmically drinking into our own darkness

the quiet deaths
of seeds and plants.

out of every possible life, the swamp is dearest.
to be the gill fibers of every quivering toad,
and set down on the water

skater's shoulders
a heavy heart.

*

стол развёрнут и кистью выметен чисто
перед каждым прибором стоит роза и плод завёрнутый
        во всё влажное
умирает вино, последний шип
и свет притупляется.

как фруктовые мушки зарождаются над открыто
        лежащим огрызком
в этом доме скоро зашевелятся хозяева.

*

the table is rolled out, swept clean with a brush
a rose for every place setting, fruit rolled in damp
the wine is dying, the last spray
as the light dulls.

and like fruit flies born of a forgotten core
the masters of the house will soon stir.

*

минута длится.
её хоронить
как косточки на будущий год.

над ней сеять сухую труху не жалея

тебя, дорогая пыльца
с прошлой вспышки,
когда тебя снова
спалило солнцем
перед холодом.

*

a minute lasts.
bury it
like fruit pits for the coming year.

sow it unsparingly with dry dust

you, dear speck of pollen
from a past explosion,
scorched once again
by the sun
before the frost.

*

мучнистое зерно
всходит только под толстым слоем тумана
густые кусты
под листьями — сгущение человека.

сгустится — станет лицо
у растения
вряд ли получится разговориться.

*

mealy grain
sprouts only under fat layers of fog
thick bushes
under leaves — a human thickening.

a plant
will thicken — become a face
but never come out of its shell.

*

высшее солнце не двинется никогда
к себе приковано идущей тяжестью.

нам солнце ходит и тянет
за собой тяжесть:

и дерево облети
и ручей уйди в землю
ещё кто под камень
и я в кожу и шерсть и волокна растений
на себя к зиме их тело взвалив.

*

the superior sun will never move
it's bound by its continuous weight.

for our sake, the sun walks and pulls
this weight along:

tree — drop your leaves
stream — hide in the earth
whoever's left — crawl under stone
and I will shoulder this skin and wool and plant fiber
for the winter, their bodies with mine

*

лучше не жми руку потому что горсть
помнит вобранную чистоту
и невечерний час входит под кожу
из ладони дует как с юга сушит глаза.

лучше проще чем что-то забыть лизать чьи-то узкие зубы
в непривычно глубоком горячем рту
и глаза влажные
и на ладонях
голый — как человек не бывает — смешанный мех.

*

better not squeeze your hand because a handful
remembers the purity imbibed
and the unfading hour enters beneath your skin
blows from your palm like a south wind dries your eyes.

better more simply than to forget, to lick someone's narrow teeth
in a strangely deep mouth
damp eyes
and palms
covered — unlike any human — in mottled fur.

*

землеройка-стервятник
роится на тусклых обломках:
она ищет и ест культурный слой

и в её светлом панцире
скользят быстрые образы

и тот кто за ними следит
из наших лиц потом
сложит почерк

*

the shrew-vulture
swarms through dark ruins
to find and eat the cultural layer

on its bright carapace
quick images glide by

whoever observes them
will use our faces
to create a new form of writing

Север

North

*

раздвоено зрение
как у змеи нюх на стороны света.

в одном окне дрожь в другом метель на стёкла давит
пресный ветер
свернул в гнёзда ветки,
хвою внутрь,
за окно яблоки.

*

forked sight
like a snake sniffs out the compass rose.

one window clatters while a snow storm presses against the panes
of another
bland wind
rolled the branches into nests,
curled the pine needles inwards,
spun the apples out the window.

*

красили лён
всем что видели и могли дотянуться,
бутонами, целиком,
но не могли:

попадались в волокнах тёмные крапины
и не росла завязь.
без одежды и жили.

но бывали согреты на теле —
пока не размешаны — краски.

*

dyed the linen
with everything they could reach,
flower buds, whole,
but it didn't take:

dark spots welled up in the fibers
and the germ didn't grow.
so, they lived on without clothing.

though warmed by their skin —
still separate — the dyes remained.

*

мимо услышанного понятный жест,
увиденного, как проснуться во сне —
ворохом отпечатки губ на руке на бумаге.

жестом трогают не воздух даже
против печали каждый день
делится множество,
когда не сказано.

*

a clear gesture beyond what was overheard,
beyond what was seen, like waking in a dream —
with a mess of misprints from a mouth
on hand and page.

they can't even touch air with this gesture
against melancholy every day
the multitudes will confide in each other,
without being told.

*

когда всё наоборот —
день темнота,
ночь неровное пламя —
ты их видишь, гостей,
лучевых, просочившихся сквозь песок, камень и глину,

через солнечный фильтр.
ненадолго, взаймы,
распадаются сразу за сомкнувшейся тенью,

и за ними секунду пахнет йодом.

*

when everything is its opposite —
day is night,
night, an uneven flame —
you see the guests,
radial, sifted through sand, stone and clay,

through the sun's filter.
momentarily, borrowed,
they break down immediately as the night closes in,

a whiff of iodine in their wake.

*

ночная перегородка между тобой и тёмным умом
сломана запахом яблока или цветка
чтобы в твой слух вошла
частыми срезами лезвием
работа холода на окне —

медленный сон больное место;
решайся, между вязкостью и разрывом.

*

the night-time barrier between you and a dark mind
is broken by the scent of an apple or a flower
and you hear the regular slicing
of the cold's blade
working into the window —

slow sleep is a painful place;
you must resolve upon the viscosity or the breach.

*

по реке полыньи, полыньи
так и сидишь почти без тела выбираешь
пару ног на сухое
как бы не провалиться
в решения хоть топор вешай, хоть ложкой греби;

сухая полынь как будто бы пахнет,
но да? если тебя уже трухой тронула оттепель

*

hole after hole in the ice along the river
and you, sitting almost bodyless, choosing
a pair of legs for dry land
trying not to fall
into decisions, enough to cut with a knife or rake in with a spoon:

like a whiff of dry wormwood
isn't it? when the thaw has already brushed you with its rot

*

выстлано белым за глазом,
а за ним только перебирать:
сколько листьев высохнет и облетит?
птицы клевали зелень: рябины нет.
белым ложится,
помню, снег — потом, теперь — память.

*

white inlaid behind the eye,
and behind the eye you can only sift through:
how many leaves will dry out and fall?
birds picking at the greenery: no rowan berries.
laid down with white,
I remember, white — then, now — memory.

*

не поздновато ли вам, красные листья на клёне.
или забыли, что не сердолики,
почти драгоценные на морозе,
и ни съесть, и ни выпить, краса голодальца,
если кому грызть зубы милее чем сладость яблока.

подержу пальцы в сугробе, и останутся дыры,
вам на память до оттепели,
а мне ненадолго красный оттиск на коже.

*

isn't it a bit late for you, red maple leaves.
or did you forget that you're not carnelians.
almost precious in the frost,
not eating or drinking, the ornament of a hunger artist,
when gnawing on his own teeth is dearer than the sweetness of an apple.

I'll hold my fingers in the snowbank, leave holes behind,
for you to remember me by until the thaw,
for me, only a brief tint of red on my skin.

*

чудеса: горестное лыко
зацвело где-то,

наверное,

пока ты тут разоряешься,
за кустами куст,

голое дерево на главном месте,
покусанный белый хлеб.

в молчащее солнечное дно
катимся —
не укатимся.

*

miracles: a sorrowful flax
bloomed somewhere,

most likely,

while here, you rant and rave,
a shrub behind shrubs,

a naked tree for a centerpiece,
a piece of bitten white bread.

we go
toward the silent sunny bottom —
we'll never leave.

*

в нашем доме свет далеко не ходит.

в три утра тебе ближе всего показали на север
а ты спишь и тень шире круга луны
из облаков и видна бы —

да с одеялом вы мученики одним миром стянуты;
столько льда на севере что не видишь и дня.

*

light doesn't make it far in our house.

north is closest at three in the morning
though you're asleep and the shadow is broader than the arc
        of the moon,
even visible from the clouds —

but you and your blanket are martyrs of the same cloth;
there's so much ice in the north you can't see the light.

Что слышно

Overheard

*

всё лопается.

будто того и ждали
у сходов в болото
с рукой на щеке жалели ухо
у вплотную в себе рвущейся древесины, одни,
но а нужна разве нам раковина для шума если в устьях
и так уже гнутся крылья у бересклета?

шевельнись — и затянется воздух;
а сожмёшься плотнее чтобы не беспокоить —
и сдует, смотри, последний звук.

*

everything bursts.

as if they were expecting it
at the descent into the swamp,
hand on cheek, nursing the ear
flush with the tight wood breaking open, alone,
do we need a seashell for sound
if the spindle tree has already bent its wings at the river mouth?

make a move — and the air will tighten;
shrink back to leave it undisturbed —
look, and the final sound will blow away.

*

главное не ошибиться в выборе горечи.

брать прогорклое
из сырой земли
безымянное
под язык где верхняя связь
целиком входит в тело,

и оно то висит — плод в пресной воде —
то роняет себя с каждой сказанной вещью
под сухое лицо.

*

the main thing is to choose the right bitterness.

take the rancid,
the nameless
from the damp earth
under your tongue where the upper link
enters the body completely,

and it either floats — like fruit in fresh water —
or falls away with every spoken thing
under a dry face.

*

чтобы выйти в ночь
надо проспать все оттенки сумерек,

среди ночи не глядя на стрелки
свериться только с их стуком

и из своих же волос на затылке
закрутить воронку.

как другую сторону ночи
волосам не увидеть своих корней.

*

to go out into the dark
you need to sleep through every shade of twilight,

don't look at the clock in the middle of the night
only check against its toll

and an eddy will curl
from the hair on the back of your neck.

like the other side of night,
hair cannot make out its own roots.

*

далеко до рассвета,
не тишина а глухота
(не глухота а немота)
приливы;
дыхание.

ночь на время
переделана в тюрьму,
за тебя кто-то пишет амнистию,

не отсидеть всю память,

ты,

прерывистый сон.

*

far from dawn,
not silence but deafness
(not deafness but muteness)
floods;
breathing.

for a while, night
is transformed into a prison,
someone is writing a pardon on your behalf,

so you don't have to serve out your memory,

you,

the faltering dream.

*

красная людская речь,

и они построили неподъёмный мост
когда хотело подняться
дно с осадком и грязью.

пока неслышно крушатся
и укрепления, и сам берег,
меня скрутило и тянет поделиться.

а с той же скоростью
для другого молча растёт коралл.

*

red human speech,

they built an insurmountable bridge
to keep the river bottom from rising
with its silt and mud.

while they silently smash
the reinforcements and the shore itself,
I was seized with a longing to confess.

at that same speed
the coral wordlessly grows for someone else.

*

как сожмёт тебя мир
откроется новое горло
будто птица свернулась в гнезде
или личинка
но распрямляется вдруг.

вдох из вчерашней погоды, выдох — в спутанных ветках,
голос — завтра,
когда от него оторвавшись
от нёба язык
ты забудешь себя.

*

when the world constricts you,
a new throat will open
like a bird curled up in its nest
or a larva
that suddenly uncoils.

breathe in yesterday's weather, breathe out — and you're
       in tangled branches,
your voice is tomorrow,
when your tongue has broken
away from the roof of your mouth,
you will forget yourself.

*

Григорию Дашевскому

ночью с грохотом мимо окна
снег летит с высоты.
может, на крыше со снегом играет в тени человек.

по стеклу в темноте расходятся дуги.
ты следишь, серый свет,
и грохоту вторя
говоришь человеку, неясный твой рот.
другу расскажешь,
тихий после падения,
снег остался ничей.

*

For Grigory Dashevsky

at night, snow roars from on high
past your window.
someone might be playing with the snow
in the shadows on the roof.

arcs radiate across the glass in the dark.
you trace them, gray light,
and you speak to this person,
echoing the roar, your mouth unclear.
you'll tell your friend the story,
and the snow, quiet after the fall,
belonged to no one.

*

Светлане Захаровой

не сложить и двух слов —
думай дважды,

придумай, как женщина
задирает подол,
как из тени
видны полосы облаков, а в нитях
сотканных взглядов
стоит пустота,

и идут в стороны свет и море,
если им приказать расступиться,
открыться, как влажным губам,
и ни слова, ни звука.

думай, как хочется кинуть
в воду камень для всплеска.
птицы думают меньше.

*

For Svetlana Zakharova

you can't kill two words with one stone —
think twice,

imagine how a woman
tucks up her skirt,
how the stripes of cloud
rise from the shadows, and in the threads,
woven with eyes,
an emptiness reigns,

and the earth and sky part,
if ordered to step away,
to open, like damp lips,
without a word or sound.

think how you long to throw
a stone into the water to hear a splash.
birds think less than that.

*

ухом к водопроводу,
ты следишь, как в стенах ссыхается ночь.
в сырых трубах ложится
ещё один слой,
это смытые с вечера разговоры,
здесь, у бессонницы в доме, в ушах стоят стены.
полная чаша,
это гостеприимное время
кормит так, что не встать.

*

ear to the waterpipe,
you listen as night shrivels inside the walls.
the evening's conversations washed away,
forming yet another layer
in the damp pipes,
only the ears have walls here, in insomnia's house.
a full chalice,
this welcoming time
feeds until you can no longer get up.

*

поди разбери шёпот собственного скелета
тихую музыку слёз.

ты может быть говоришь с ущельем
под дверью?
с тайной
в немытом углу.

только в ушах есть стены
и льётся свет
за перегородкой.

*

just try to make out the whisper of your own skeleton
the quiet music of tears.

maybe you're talking to the crack
under the door?
to the mystery
in an unwashed corner.

only ears have walls
with light that pours
beyond their borders.

*

в целые петли вдень пальцы
если завален проём если в окне нет новой
нет старой луны.

за плотно сдвинутыми скобами
щель
что либо читают под лампой;
либо разлили полный стакан;
 не успел и попить а уже и услали
за камнями за плечи.

боль в глазах от того как привык к темноте
что чужой против света
на твою тень набросив свою за спиной весит больше чем дом.

если петли сцепились как цепь,
ты сдвинешь на половину звука
и лист и стекло.
на половину звука, это целая ночь.

*

thread your fingers into loops
if the opening has collapsed, if there is no new
or old moon in the window.

behind the tight clamps
a crack
either they're reading by lamplight;
or spilled the whole glass;
hardly took a sip before they sent him packing
back beyond the stones.

his eyes burn, he's so used to the dark,
alien to light
dragging his shadow with yours weighs more than a house.

if the loops had formed a chain,
you'd move the leaf and glass
for half a sound.
half a sound makes a whole night.

*

как найдёшь в лесу спящего,
отними ему руки от век,
откати с колен камни.
думай ему
то, что есть.
положи на себя его груз,
отнесёшь к морю.

спящий носит на выдохе
тёмный покой.
он возьмёт с тебя слово
оглушёнными ночью ушами
и вернёт, рак в ракушку,
пространство в твой жадно
вдыхающий рот.

пусть память,
когда откатилась,
возвращает приливы листве,
под деревьями слышен
и маленький шум.

*

when you find the sleeper in the forest,
remove his hands from his lids,
roll the stones from his lap.
think to him
what is.
take his burden upon yourself,
and carry it to the sea.

the sleeper breathes out
a dark peace.
he will take speech from you
with ears deafened by night
and return space, crab to shell,
to your greedily
breathing mouth.

let memory,
when it has rolled back,
return tides to the leaves,
even a small sound can be heard
under the trees.

Часть полноты

Part of a Whole

*

озеро моет пеной прозрачную воду с высот
и на равнине перед закатом тесно как горы растут пустырные тени

дальше мы спим
солнце ходит лунатик

*

the lake washes the clear water with foam from above
and wasteland shadows crowd the plain like mountains before sunset

we keep sleeping
the sun a somnambulist

*

н.с.

1.

морская звезда от рождения распята.
ты потому на неё пятками встала
чтобы руки раскинуть
и в глубоких глазницах глазам
от рождения темно,
и задумчивый рот сжат в ответ глубине.

2.

напоминание
о внутреннем городе —

запах залитых нечистой водой
подземных ходов
ржавчины
крючьев

были когда-то нужны,

*

n.s.

1.

from birth, a sea star is crucified.
you stepped on it with a heel
to stretch your arms outward,
eyes furrowed in deep sockets
that perceive darkness from birth,
the pensive mouth pursed to the depths.

2.

a reminder
of the city inside —

the smell of underground passageways
flooded with dirty water,
rusted
hooked

once necessary

теперь —
как цветная роспись по телу —
только чтобы не забывать

о внешнем городе.

now —
like a colorful painting the length of a body —
that only precludes forgetting

about the city outside.

*

некто рассматривает
полёты рваных краёв
над открытым проёмом.

ты, не имущий одежд,
повязываешь
бесполезными лентами пустоту.

никто!
большая радость
когда
ничего не близится.

как мой брат,
никому не угодно
управлять ходьбой.

*

someone examines
the flights of torn edges
over an open aperture.

you, poor of vestment,
tie up
the emptiness with useless ribbon.

nobody!
the great joy
when
nothing approaches.

like my brother,
nobody wishes
to command his own steps.

*

Леониду Швабу

не глуха полнота если край
надо мной как на дороге камнем платье поднять.

я растягиваю кусок мокрого полотна
рву поворотную нить.

так же и кожа ткань.
полнота зарастает сорным исподним
чёрным в ирисе чёрным зрачком в анемоне.

*

To Leonid Schwab

is the whole deaf, if the hem of a dress
lifts above me as I lie in the road like a stone.

I stretch a piece of wet canvas
I tear the main thread.

skin is also like cloth in this way.
the whole becomes entwined with the weedy black underside
in the iris of the black pupil inside of an anemone.

*

Владимиру Богомякову

год за годом
скручивается небо
новыми видами облаков
в самый глубокий колодец воронкой;

в ней и чёрная тяжесть
и светлая влага

невыносимо такое сплетение

только сдвиг и наклон
водят мимо отчаяния.

*

To Vladimir Bogomyakov

year after year
the sky twists
with new types of clouds
into the deepest well like a funnel;

there is a dark heaviness
and a bright mist inside

unbearable, this weaving

only upheaval and decline
guide you past despair.

*

это когда стараешься
только вполсилы
выходит вода из камня,
ты — портной,
вода — слеза,
камень — сыр.

а пробеги по заброшенному
мосту над ржавой
железной дорогой;

по обугленной балке
на детской площадке
под треугольными скатами в теремке.

тогда и безлесный пространства клочок
будет жгучий
и молния с неба.

*

it's only when
you're half trying
that water seeps from stone,
you are the tailor,
water is the fallen tear,
the stone is the cheese.

slip by on the abandoned
bridge over the rusty
railroad;

on the sooty beam
on the playground
over the little house's pitched roof.

then even the treeless scrap of field
will be burning
as lightning cracks from the sky.

*

царь своей головы
созерцает простор,
ход планеты
из стороны времени в сторону времени
по горячим следам расширяется и догорает закат.

голова опускается вслед,
и из этого неба
к нему
сходит седьмое небо.

*

the king of his own head
contemplates the vastness,
planetary movement
from time over time
the sunset widens and burns out along the hot tracks.

the head lowers in kind,
and toward it
from that sky
the seventh heaven sets.

*

сердце — убывающий маятник,
вода — тоже, но прибывает.

можно
приспособиться к дыханию, верху и низу,
но как — к постоянной дуге глазных яблок,
как — если кривизна не сходит с глаз?

день и ночь — маятник,
изогнутый в сторону теперь уже тёмного прилива.

*

the heart is a receding pendulum,
so is water, but it rises.

it's possible
to adapt to breathing, above and below,
but how do you adapt to the constant arc of the eye,
how — if eyeballs can't shake their curvature?

day and night — a pendulum,
swung toward the already darkened tide.

*

проповедь на пустыре к чему-то засохшему.
исповедь лицом вплотную к стене.
ты обращаешься ко мне?

— камень,
остывший жар,
когда вынесло из-под земли
на солнечную сторону.

*

a sermon in the desert to something withered.
a confession with your face against the wall.
are you talking to me?

— stone,
heat gone cold,
taken from underground
to the sunlit side.

*

1.

хотелось бы уже теперь прославиться
изобретением несгораемого угля,
несметной золы,
огнераздела на все стороны и напротив,
одомашнить погоду или с ней одичать,
лишь бы вместе.

уже сейчас,
разменявшись на ветер,
заплатить за тление,
если мало грозного воздуха дали взаймы
лесному, степному
живущему.

2.

где-то в самом равнинном озере
скапливается перемена участи земле
или она утяжеляется
и удаляется внутрь

или бродит в ней под корой бывшее дерево
как у безумного память?

*

1.

it'd be nice to have some recognition by now
for the invention of fire-proof coal,
infinite soot,
firesheds everywhere,
to domesticate the weather or run wild with it,
as long as we're together.

even now,
wind is exchanged
to pay for glowing embers,
when too little thunderous air is on loan
to the forest dweller, the steppe wanderer,
the living.

2.

somewhere in the shallowest lake
the earth's change in fate is accumulating
or growing heavier
and withdrawing

or does a former tree wander inside its bark
like a memory in a mind gone mad?

пыль выветривается.
после мир окажется плоским,
мы смешно ошибались.

что делать? молить
о расширении взгляда
на время земли.

3.

долиной может быть и подземное море,
если ровные существа его населяют,
если плоть стала местом.

dust blows away.
after, the world turns flat,
we were hilariously mistaken.

what now? pray
for a wider gaze
toward this season of the earth.

3.

even an underground sea can be a valley,
if steady beings settle it,
if flesh has become place.

*

волны стучат о сердце,
это приступы тумана,
стыд за необъявленные задержки,
между приливами,
много, огрехи.

чтобы занять себя,
можно вытравливать пятна
в чистом воздухе
чистым бездействием.

*

waves knock against the heart,
attacks of fog,
the shame of unannounced delays,
between tides,
so many, flaws.

you can keep yourself busy
by expunging spots
in pure air
with pure inaction.

*

1.

если гусеница проглотит
блуждающий камень
и замкнётся началом к концу,

камень будет ходить в ней
пока не настанет ей время переродиться,

и тогда он положит начало
их календарю.

2.

белая гусеница
ест себя насухо
а икра не может лосося изнутри заполнить всего.

всё в своих нитях
время врастает в свой поворот
это повод тебе измениться.

*

1.

if the caterpillar swallows
a vagrant stone
and the beginning comes to an end,

the stone will move within her
until the right moment for rebirth,

and that birth will mark the beginning
of their calendars.

2.

a white caterpillar
eats itself dry
and roe cannot fill the whole salmon.

in its very fibers,
time grows into its reversal
a call for you to change.

Translator's Afterword | Alex Niemi

In 2015, I was working at a school in Vladimir, Russia, and had decided to spend my winter vacation in Saint Petersburg. The sun barely rose in the sky, and I spent most of that month's salary at "Poryadok Slov," a well-known bookstore among Petersburg intellectuals and writers. Of all the books I brought home from the trip, Anna Glazova's *For the Shrew* stood out—I read the entire book in my third-class bunk on the night train back to Moscow. I was entranced by her exploration of nature, time, space, and consciousness in tight, unrhymed lines that interweave philosophy and poetry. I reached out to Glazova a year or so later, and we began collaborating on translations. She is a generous reader, and an experienced translator, who has brought Paul Celan, Unica Zürn, Robert Walser, Franz Kafka, and Walter Benjamin from German into Russian, and she worked with me on the translation of her work into English, a language she also speaks fluently. It has been wonderful to correspond with her over the years, trading ideas for the translations as well as pictures of birds and flowers.

For the Shrew won the Andrei Bely Prize in 2013. This prize is the oldest independent literature prize in Russia, and it was founded in 1978 by leading figures of Russian samizdat, or literature written underground in defiance of the Soviet State. Today, the prize recognizes work in fiction, poetry, humanities research, translation, and service to Russian literature. Receiving the prize is a major honor in Russian letters, and Glazova had already been shortlisted twice for her poetry collections *Even the Water* and *The Loop. Unhalved* before her win in 2013. Glazova is also an active member of the Russophone poetry scene. She has acted as a judge for the Arkadii Dragomoshchenko Prize for young poets, and she is on the editorial board for the literary journal *Daydream*. She dedicates much of her time to supporting other writers in addition to her own poetry and scholarly work.

*

Fellow poet Polina Barskova has described Glazova as "a microscope poet," whose work zooms in on the tiniest details of the natural world—bees, flowers, the titular shrew—and develops her observations into philosophical ruminations. Scholar Luba Golburt describes Glazova's work as "a thoughtful recalibration" of the Russian nature lyric, "blurring the boundaries between animacy and inanimacy, animality and humanity."[1] Because of this blurring, I often feel disembodied when I'm reading *For the Shrew*, as if I've finally learned to dissolve into the forest, or achieved a state of vibrant stillness. Another scholar, Anna Vichkitova, describes it as Glazova's ability to "[destabilize] humanness," and that in her poetry language is more than "a mere system of signs to share information between humans."[2] For example, she presents us with an imagined creature, the "shrew-vulture" (p. 57) and then expands on the wider implications of this animal's influence on humanity's ability to communicate. In the poem, the "shrew-vulture" is the progenitor of writing, the inspiration for humans to create a new form of communication. In Glazova's work, it's the animals

1. Luba Golburt, "The Ethics of Grammar in Anna Glazova's Nature Lyric," *Neuere Lyrik. Interkulturelle und interdisziplinäre Studien* 8.2 (2020): 267.

2. Anna Vichkitova, "Poetry of Anna Glazova: Attempting to Reimagine Humanness and Otherness," (unpublished manuscript, July 19, 2021), typescript.

who have something to teach the humans, if only we can learn to observe and give up our anthropocentric predispositions.

Another aspect of Glazova's writing that separates her from many of her contemporaries is her life-long work with German literature. Glazova's expansive knowledge is due to her work as a translator and her active scholarly practice. Though originally trained as an architect in Berlin, Glazova went on to earn a Ph.D. in Comparative Literary Studies at Northwestern University where she defended her thesis on the work of Paul Celan and Osip Mandelstam. Glazova has cited Celan as having a large impact on her poetry, and we can pinpoint other examples of German influence in *For the Shrew*, such as the poem "of a full life" (p. 11) which presents a thematic play on Friedrich Hölderlin's "Half of Life." Here is Hölderlin's poem as translated by David Young:

Half of Life

The land with yellow pears
and full of wild roses,
hangs there in the lake
behind you, lovely swans,
and you are drunk with kisses as
you dip your graceful heads
in holy sober water.

Where am I going to find
come winter, all these flowers?
And where will the sunshine be

and earth's shade to go with it?
The walls stand there before me,
speechless and cold; the wind
rattles the weathervane.[3]

In the translation of Hölderlin, we can see the inspiration for Glazova's images, such as the "yellow pears" and "wild roses," and Glazova increases the sense of tension in the poem with the prospect of winter from the very beginning of her version, with plants that "barely hold on" and "won't hold out." I read a level of existential threat in Glazova's version that suggests a commentary on climate change, relating Hölderlin's imagery to a contemporary concern, particularly with the clock at the end instead of the weathervane, as if we were running out of time. The closeness of the two poems also feels like an act of experimental translation to me, and there were more than a few times in discussing Glazova's poems with her that I wished I had stronger German, so that I could better understand the interplay between her translation practice and her writing.

*

People often talk about loss in translation. I view translation as a generative creative writing process, and Glazova and I both approached our work on *For the Shrew* with this mindset. There are certainly moments when the definitions of words or the peculiarities of idioms don't line up across

3. Friedrich Hölderlin, "Half of Life," trans. David Young, *Plume Poetry* 39 (September 2014), https://plumepoetry.com/half-of-life/.

languages, but these are often, for me, the most exciting and creatively engaging parts of the translation process. For this project, I would initially begin the translation alone—experimenting with different iterations of lines, reining in my own poetic impulses, leaving translations aside for long periods in the hope that I could revisit them with fresh eyes—and then I would send drafts to Glazova with questions. She told me early in the process that she would like to be involved with the translation, and after my second draft, we would collaborate on the third and subsequent drafts.

"before dawn, light crashes . . ." (p. 19) presents one of the creative solutions we devised for dealing with an idiom. At the end of the poem in Russian, there is a play on the expression "отлегло от сердца" which literally means to have one's heart unburdened, or to be relieved. A literal rendition of the last line in Russian would be "knowing that your life has now been unburdened of everyone." The closest idiom in English to the original expression is "to have a load taken off one's mind," but I didn't feel that the expression could be adequately molded to the idea of people you have lost contact with. I tried to think of similar ideas in English that would involve people leaving, and so came up with, "left your mind at ease," and then "everyone has left your life at ease."

Also, when you become familiar enough with an author's work, you can intuit places for new wordplay in English not in the original, but implicit within the boundaries of the author's style. In the following example, the last three lines of the Russian poem "мучнистое зерно" (p. 50) read literally something like "will thicken — will become a face/in the plant/but will probably never start talking." When I read this line, I immediately thought of the expression in English, "to come out of one's shell" as expressing the idea of starting to speak with nature imagery:

> a plant
> will thicken — become a face
> but never come out of its shell.

I added the ending and sent the draft to Glazova as usual, without any preamble, to see what she would think. She wrote back that that was her favorite translation of the ten or so I'd sent her. This is an example of a poetic opportunity being "found" in translation. Glazova and I were both excited about this addition to the poem in English and felt it was very much in line with her poetic voice.

Acknowledgments

Many thanks to Zephyr Press for bringing these poems into English and for supporting poetry in translation. The poems in this volume of translations make up around half the original work and were chosen in conjunction with the author and publisher. I am grateful to Jim Kates and Cris Mattison for their comments on the translations, as well as to my former colleague at the University of Iowa, Anna Kolesnikova Dyer, for her lively conversation and translation ideas. Earlier versions of some of these poems were published in *Columbia Journal* and *The Café Review*. Thank you to the editors of those journals.

All my love and gratitude to Greg for reading drafts, listening to me talk about translation (even though he's a mathematician), and going on a thousand walks in the woods.